Christopher Shinn

Methuen Drama

Published by Methuen Drama 2008

1 3 5 7 9 10 8 6 4 2

Methuen Drama
A & C Black Publishers Limited
36 Soho Square
London W1D 3QY
www.acblack.com

ISBN 978 1 408 11268 7

A CIP catalogue record for this book is available from
the British Library

Typeset by Country Setting, Kingsdown, Kent
Printed and bound in Great Britain by
CPI Cox & Wyman, Reading, RG1 8EX

This book is produced using paper that is made from wood grown
in managed, sustainable forests. It is natural, renewable and recyclable.
The logging and manufacturing processes conform to the environmental
regulations of the country of origin.

ROYAL COURT

Royal Court Theatre presents

NOW OR LATER

by **Christopher Shinn**

First performance at the Royal Court Jerwood Theatre Downstairs, Sloane Square, London
on 3 September 2008.

NOW OR LATER

by **Christopher Shinn**

Cast in order of appearance
Marc **Adam James**
Matt **Domhnall Gleeson**
John **Eddie Redmayne**
Jessica **Nancy Crane**
Tracy **Pamela Nomvete**
John Sr **Matthew Marsh**

THE LEARNING CENTRES
TOWN CENTRE CAMPUS
EASTWOOD LANE
ROTHERHAM S65 1EG

Director **Dominic Cooke**
Designer **Hildegard Bechtler**
Lighting Designer **Charles Balfour**
Sound Designer **Ian Dickinson**
Assistant Director **Des Kennedy***
Assistant Designer **Luke Smith**
Casting Director **Amy Ball**
Production Manager **Paul Handley**
Stage Manager **Richard Llewelyn**
Deputy Stage Manager **Fran O'Donnell**
Assistant Stage Manager **Rebecca Bailey**
Costume Supervisor **Iona Kenrick**
Dialect Coach **Penny Dyer**
Fight Director **Terry King**
Stage Management Work Placement **Ralph Buchanan**
Set Built by **Miraculous Engineering**
Set Painted by **Charlotte Gainey, Natasha Shepherd**

*The assistant director is a participant on Rough Magic Theatre Company's AIB SEEDS Programme.

The Royal Court and Stage Management wish to thank the following for their help with this production:
Dr Jonathan Bell, Michael Boyd, Jeanie O'Hare, Dr Bernard Roberts, Peter Wilby.

THE COMPANY

CHRISTOPHER SHINN (Writer)

FOR THE ROYAL COURT: Dying City, Four, Other People, Where Do We Live.

OTHER PLAYS INCLUDE: The Coming World, What Didn't Happen, On the Mountain.

Christopher's plays have been produced at the Royal Court, Manhattan Theatre Club, Playwrights Horizons, the Vineyard Theatre, South Coast Rep, and Soho Theatre, among others.

AWARDS INCLUDE: An Obie in Playwriting and a Guggenheim Fellowship in Playwriting.

CHARLES BALFOUR (Lighting Designer)

FOR THE ROYAL COURT: The Ugly One, Country Music.

RECENT THEATRE CREDITS INCLUDE: The English Game and Angels in America (Headlong); I'll Be the Devil (RSC/Tricycle); Duchess of Malfi, Hedda Gabler, Don Quixote (West Yorkshire Playhouse); The Glee Club (New Vic); Blythe Spirit (Watford Palace); The Flint Street Nativity, The Tempest (Liverpool Playhouse); A Doll's House, Christmas Carol, Son of Man (Northern Stage); Cleansed (Arcola/ Oxford Stage Co.); Hair, Woyzeck, Witness (Gate); Baby Doll, Thérèse Raquin, Bash (Citizens Glasgow); Through the Leaves (Southwark Playhouse/West End); Cake, Grace (Jade/BAC/Birmingham Rep/tour); Ghost City (Sgript Cymru).

DANCE INCLUDES: 25 works for Richard Alston Dance Company (Sadlers Wells/New York/worldwide); Eden/Eden (Wayne McGregor/Stuttgart Ballet/San Francisco Ballet); Bloom (Aletta Collins/Rambert Dance Co.); Sheer Bravado (Richard Alston/Ballet Theatre Munich); Four Seasons (Oliver Hindle/Birmingham Royal Ballet); White, Women and Memory (Rosemary Butcher/Tate Modern Turbine Hall/Queen Elizabeth Hall/worldwide); Charge, About Face (Martin Lawrance/Sadlers Wells/tour); Silent Rhythms (Matthew Hawkins/ROH Linbury); Dancing Attendance (Rambert); and many others.

MUSIC INCLUDES: Silence, Night and Dreams (Zbigniew Preisner – Barbican/Herodian, Athens); Saul (Opera North); The Marriage of Figaro (Guildhall School); The Birds (The Opera Group); Jordan Town (Errollyn Wallen, ROH); Writing to Vermeer (London Sinfonietta, South Bank); Thimble Rigging (Royal Festival Hall).

Charles began designing lights in 1987 as a member of the Shadow Syndicate.

HILDEGARD BECHTLER (Designer)

FOR THE ROYAL COURT: The Seagull, Krapp's Last Tape, My Name is Rachel Corrie (and West End/ Edinburgh Festival/New York), Forty Winks, The Sweetest Swing in Baseball, Blood, Terrorism, Blasted, The Changing Room.

OTHER THEATRE INCLUDES: The Hour We Knew Nothing of Each Other, Harper Regan, The Hothouse, Thérèse Raquin, Exiles, Iphigenia at Aulis, The Merchant of Venice, Richard II, King Lear (National); Rosmersholm (Almeida); The Crucible (RSC/West End); All About My Mother, Richard II (Old Vic); By the Bog of Cats (Wyndham's); The Goat or Who is Sylvia? (Almeida/West End); The Master Builder (Albery); Primo (National/Broadway); La Maison de Poupée (Theatre de l'Europe, Paris); Footfalls (Garrick); The St. Pancras Project (LIFT); Electra (RSC/Riverside/Bobigny, Paris); Hedda Gabler (Abbey, Dublin/Playhouse, London); Coriolanus (Salzburg Festival).

OPERA INCLUDES: War and Peace, Boris Gudunov, Peter Grimes, Lohengrin, The Bacchae (ENO); Lady Macbeth of Mtsensk (Sydney Opera House); Paul Bunyan (ROH); Les Dialogues des Carmelites (Japan/ Paris Opera): Simon Boccanegra, Peter Grimes (Staatsoper, Munich); Don Carlos, Wozzeck, Katya Kabanova (Opera North); La Cenerentola, Don Giovanni (Glyndebourne); La Wally (Bregenz Festival/Amsterdam Musik Theatre); The Ring Cycle (Scottish Opera/Edinburgh Festival); and most recently Dido and Aeneas (La Scala, Milan).

FILM AND TELEVISION INCLUDES: Primo, The Merchant of Venice, Richard II, The Wasteland, Hedda Gabler, Coming Up Roses, Business as Usual.

DOMINIC COOKE (Director)

FOR THE ROYAL COURT: War & Peace/Fear & Misery, Rhinoceros, The Pain and The Itch, Other People, Fireface, Spinning into Butter, Redundant, Fucking Games, Plasticine, The People are Friendly, This is a Chair, Identical Twins.

OTHER THEATRE INCLUDES: Pericles, The Winter's Tale, The Crucible, Postcards from America, As You Like It, Macbeth, Cymbeline, The Malcontent (RSC); By the Bog of Cats (Wyndham's); The Eccentricities of a Nightingale (Gate, Dublin); Arabian Nights (Young Vic/UK & world tours/New Victory Theatre, New York); The Weavers, Hunting Scenes From Lower Bavaria (Gate); The Bullet (Donmar); Afore Night Come, Entertaining Mr Sloane (Clwyd); The Importance of Being Earnest (Atlantic Theatre Festival, Canada); Caravan (National Theatre of Norway); My Mother Said I Never Should (Oxford Stage Co./Young Vic); Kiss of the Spider Woman (Bolton Octagon); Of Mice and Men (Nottingham Playhouse); Autogeddon (Assembly Rooms).

OPERA INCLUDES: The Magic Flute (WNO); I Capuleti E I Montecchi, La Bohème (Grange Park Opera).

AWARDS INCLUDE: Laurence Olivier Awards for Best Director and Best Revival for The Crucible; TMA Award for Arabian Nights; Fringe First Award for Autogeddon; Manchester Evening News Award for The Marriage of Figaro.

Associate director of the Royal Court 1999–2002, associate director of the RSC 2002–2006, assistant director RSC 1992–1993.

Dominic is Artistic Director of the Royal Court.

NANCY CRANE (Jessica)

FOR THE ROYAL COURT: The Sweetest Swing in Baseball, Our Late Night, The Strip.

OTHER THEATRE INCLUDES: Chains of Dew, Trifles (Orange Tree); Dis-Orientations (Riverside); Girl in the Goldfish Bowl, Six Degrees of Separation (Sheffield Crucible); The Price (tour); Habitat (Manchester Royal Exchange); A Wedding Story (tour); Absolution (BAC); Angels in America/Perestroika, Millennium Approaches (National); Walk on Lake Erie (Finborough); Threesome (Gay Sweatshop); Oh Hell! (Lyric Studio); Last of the Red Hot Lovers (Derby Playhouse); Caligula (Boulevard Theatre); Never the Sinner (Belgrade Theatre).

TELEVISION INCLUDES: Cambridge Spies, Strike Force, Last Days of Patton, 92 Grosvenor Street.

FILM INCLUDES: The Dark Knight, Road to Guantanamo, The Machinist, Sky Captain and the World of Tomorrow, The Fourth Protocol.

RADIO INCLUDES: Wit, The Ideal Heroine, Ice Blond, The Joy Luck Club, The Weight of Water.

IAN DICKINSON (Sound Designer)

FOR THE ROYAL COURT: Gone Too Far!, Rhinoceros, My Child, The Eleventh Capital, The Seagull, Krapp's Last Tape, Piano/Forte, Rock 'n' Roll (& West End/Broadway), Motortown, Rainbow Kiss, The Winterling, Alice Trilogy, Fewer Emergencies, Way to Heaven, The Woman Before, Stoning Mary (& Drum Theatre, Plymouth), Breathing Corpses, Wild East, Dumb Show, Shining City (& Gate, Dublin), Lucky Dog, Blest Be the Tie (with Talawa), Ladybird, Notes on Falling Leaves, Loyal Women, The Sugar Syndrome, Blood, Playing the Victim (with Told By an Idiot), Fallout, Flesh Wound, Hitchcock Blonde (& Lyric), Black Milk, Crazyblackmuthafuckin'self, Caryl Churchill Shorts, Push Up, Fucking Games, Herons.

OTHER THEATRE INCLUDES: Harper Regan, The Hothouse, Pillars of the Community (National); Testing the Echo, King Of Hearts (Out of Joint); Love and Money (Young Vic); Much Ado About Nothing (redesign, RSC/Novello); A Few Good Men (Haymarket); Dr Faustus (Chichester Festival Theatre); The Magic Carpet (Lyric Hammersmith); Port, As You Like It, Poor Superman, Martin Yesterday, Fast Food, Coyote Ugly (Manchester Royal Exchange); Night of the Soul (RSC/Barbican); Eyes of the Kappa (Gate); Crime & Punishment in Dalston (Arcola); Search & Destroy (New End); The Whore's Dream (RSC/Edinburgh).

Ian is Head of Sound at the Royal Court.

DOMHNALL GLEESON (Matt)

THEATRE INCLUDES: Macbeth (Siren Productions); Great Expectations, American Buffalo (Gate, Dublin); Lieutenant of Inishmore (West End/Broadway); Chimps (Liverpool Playhouse); Well of the Saints (Druid Theatre Co.); She Stoops to Conquer (Abbey, Dublin).

TELEVISION INCLUDES: The Last Furlong, Rebel Heart.

FILM INCLUDES: A Dog Year, Studs, Stars, Boy Eats Girl, Six Shooter.

ADAM JAMES (Marc)

FOR THE ROYAL COURT: My Child.

OTHER THEATRE INCLUDES: Rabbit (Trafalgar Studios/59E59, New York); French Without Tears (English Touring Theatre); The Importance of Being Earnest (No 1 tour); Original Sin (Sheffield Crucible); Time and the Conways, Snake in Fridge, King Lear, Poor Superman (Manchester Royal Exchange); Glass Menagerie (Minerva); Chimes at Midnight (Chichester); Unseen Hand, Lone Star, Private Wars (Bristol Old Vic); A View from the Bridge (Theatre Royal, York); Tamburlaine the Great (RSC); Coriolanus (NYT).

TELEVISION INCLUDES: The Grinning Man – Jonathan Creek Christmas Special, Hustle V, Hotel Babylon IV, Wired, Secret Diary of a Call Girl II, Sleep with Me, Bonekickers, Harley Street, Ashes to Ashes, Extras Christmas Special, Sold, The Commander, The Amazing Mrs Pritchard, Waking the Dead, Judge John Deed, Desperados, The Jewish Revolt, Shiny Shiny Bright New Hole in My Heart, Lovesoup, Casualty, England Expects, Reversals, As If, Trust, After Hours, The Lost Battalion, Murder on the Orient Express, Band of Brothers, I Saw You, Life of the Party, Tenth Kingdom, Let Them Eat Cake, Silent Witness, Island II, Sharpe's Regiment, Cold Lazarus.

FILM INCLUDES: Last Chance Harvey, Broken Lines, Mother of Tears, Road to Guantanamo, De-Lovely, Prima Dammi Un Baccio, A Family Man, Three Blind Mice, It's Not You It's Me, High Heels and Low Life, Gregory's 2 Girls, Forbidden Territory.

DES KENNEDY (Assistant Director)

AS DIRECTOR, THEATRE INCLUDES: The Last Days of Judas Iscariot (Queens Studio); Gleaming Dark (Trafalgar Studios); Blocked (Lyric); Scenes from the Big Picture (Solas-Nua, Washington D.C.); The Missing (twentyfivebelfast); Twelfth Night (Waterfront Studio); Barren (Old Vic New Voices, 24 Hour Plays); The Bridge of San Luis-Rey (YMT:UK); Sfilata di Cartone Animato (Teatro Senza Frontiere, Milan); The Laramie Project (Sunday Times NSDF'04).

AS ASSISTANT DIRECTOR, THEATRE INCLUDES: Crooked (Bush); Dream Me a Winter (Old Vic, Celebrity 24 Hour Plays); Monte Cristo (YMT:UK Birmingham Hippodrome); The Elixir of Love (WNO).

Des is a participant on Rough Magic Theatre Company's AIB SEEDS Programme.

MATTHEW MARSH (John Sr)

THEATRE INCLUDES: A Prayer for My Daughter (Young Vic); Glengarry Glen Ross (Apollo); The Lightning Play (Almeida); The Overwhelming (National with Out of Joint/tour); The Exonerated (Riverside); The Goat or Who Is Sylvia? (Almeida/West End); Us and Them (Hampstead); A Buyer's Market (Bush); The Little Foxes (Donmar); Conversations After a Burial (Almeida/tour); Copenhagen (National/West End).

TELEVISION INCLUDES: How Not to Live Your Life, Lewis, The Street, Marie Lloyd, Spooks, The Commander, Service, Murphy's Law, Belonging, Return of the Dancing Master, Wall of Silence, Real Men, Murder in Mind.

FILM INCLUDES: The Endgame, Land of the Blind, An American Haunting, Bad Company, Miranda, Spygame, Quicksand, O Jerusalem.

PAMELA NOMVETE (Tracy)

FOR THE ROYAL COURT: Marching for Fausa, Leavetaking.

OTHER THEATRE INCLUDES: Talking in Tongues (Lyric Hammersmith); Racing Demon – The David Hare Trilogy, Fuente Overture (National); Sanctuary (Joint Stock); A Raisin in the Sun (Durban Playhouse); The Good Woman of Sharkville, Nothing but the Truth (Market Theatre, S. Africa); Going to St Ives (Peter Turin Theatre, S. Africa); Salvation (South African tour).

TELEVISION INCLUDES: Behind the Badge, Generations, Born Free: New Adventure, EastEnders.

FILM INCLUDES: Sometimes in April, Zulu Love Letter, A Reasonable Man, Human Time Bomb, Orion's Key.

AWARDS INCLUDE: Fespaco Film Best Actress Award 2005 for Zulu Love Letter; Naledi Best Supporting Actress Award 2003 for Nothing but the Truth; Durban Stage Best Actress Award 2000 for A Raisin in the Sun; Duku Duku Best Actress Award 1999 for Generations.

EDDIE REDMAYNE (John)

THEATRE INCLUDES: Hecuba (Donmar); The Goat or Who is Sylvia? (Almeida/West End); Master Harold and the Boys (Liverpool Everyman); Twelfth Night (Globe at the Middle Temple).

TELEVISION INCLUDES: Tess of the D'Urbervilles, Elizabeth I, In Search of Shakespeare.

FILM INCLUDES: Powder Blue, Yellow Handkerchief, Savage Grace, The Other Boleyn Girl, Elizabeth – The Golden Age, The Good Shepherd, Like Minds.

AWARDS INCLUDE: 2005 Critics' Circle Theatre Award for Outstanding Newcomer; 2004 Evening Standard Award for Outstanding Newcomer.

20 Nov 2008 – 10 Jan 2009

JERWOOD THEATRE DOWNSTAIRS

wig out!

by Tarell Alvin McCraney

Bringing to glorious, vivid life, a riotous, defiant drag
queen subculture. Stylish people only need apply!

THE ENGLISH STAGE COMPANY
AT THE ROYAL COURT

'For me the theatre is really a religion or way of life. You must decide what you feel the world is about and what you want to say about it, so that everything in the theatre you work in is saying the same thing ... A theatre must have a recognisable attitude. It will have one, whether you like it or not.'

George Devine, first artistic director of the English Stage Company: notes for an unwritten book.

photo: Stephen Cummiskey

As Britain's leading national company dedicated to new work, the Royal Court Theatre produces new plays of the highest quality, working with writers from all backgrounds, and addressing the problems and possibilities of our time.

"The Royal Court has been at the centre of British cultural life for the past 50 years, an engine room for new writing and constantly transforming the theatrical culture" Stephen Daldry

Since its foundation in 1956, the Royal Court has presented premieres by almost every leading contemporary British playwright, from John Osborne's *Look Back in Anger* to Caryl Churchill's *A Number* and Tom Stoppard's *Rock 'n' Roll*. Just some of the other writers to have chosen the Royal Court to premiere their work include Edward Albee, John Arden, Samuel Beckett, Edward Bond, Jez Butterworth, Martin Crimp, Ariel Dorfman, Christopher Hampton, David Hare, Eugène Ionesco, Ann Jellicoe, Terry Johnson, Sarah Kane, David Mamet, Martin McDonagh, Conor McPherson, Mark Ravenhill, Wole Soyinka, Polly Stenham, David Storey, debbie tucker green, Arnold Wesker and Roy Williams.

"It is risky to miss a production there" Financial Times

In addition to its full-scale productions, the Royal Court also facilitates international work at a grass roots level, developing exchanges which bring young writers to Britain and sending British writers, actors and directors to work with artists around the world. The Royal Court Young Writers' Programme also works to develop new voices with their bi-annual Festival and year-round development work for writers under the age of 26.

"Yes, the Royal Court is on a roll. Yes, Dominic Cooke has just the genius and kick that this venue needs... It's fist-bitingly exciting." Independent

PROGRAMME SUPPORTERS

The Royal Court (English Stage Company Ltd) receives its principal funding from Arts Council England, London. It is also supported financially by a wide range of private companies, charitable and public bodies, and earns the remainder of its income from the box office and its own trading activities.

The Genesis Foundation supports the Royal Court's work with International Playwrights.

The Jerwood Charity supports new plays by new playwrights through the Jerwood New Playwrights series.

The Artistic Director's Chair is supported by a lead grant from The Peter Jay Sharp Foundation, contributing to the activities of the Artistic Director's office. Over the past ten years the BBC has supported the Gerald Chapman Fund for directors.

ROYAL COURT DEVELOPMENT BOARD
John Ayton
Anthony Burton
Sindy Caplan (Vice-Chair)
Cas Donald
Allie Esiri
Celeste Fenichel
Stephen Marquardt
Emma Marsh
Mark Robinson
William Russell (Chair)

PUBLIC FUNDING
Arts Council England, London
British Council
London Challenge

CHARITABLE DONATIONS
American Friends of the Royal Court Theatre
Bulldog Prinsep Theatrical Fund
Gerald Chapman Fund
Columbia Foundation
The Sidney & Elizabeth Corob Charitable Trust
Cowley Charitable Trust
The Edmond de Rothschild Foundation*
The Dorset Foundation
The D'oyly Carte Charitable Trust
E*TRADE Financial
Esmée Fairbairn Foundation
The Edwin Fox Foundation
Francis Finlay*
The Garfield Weston Foundation
Genesis Foundation
Haberdashers' Company
Jerwood Charitable Foundation
John Thaw Foundation
Kudos Film and Televisoin
Lloyds TSB Foundation for England and Wales
Dorothy Loudon Foundation*

Lynn Foundation
John Lyon's Charity
The Laura Pels Foundation*
The Martin Bowley Charitable Trust
Paul Hamlyn Foundation
The Peggy Ramsay Foundation
Quercus Charitable Trust
Jerome Robbins Foundation*
Rose Foundation
Royal College of Psychiatrists
The Royal Victoria Hall Foundation
The Peter Jay Sharp Foundation*
Sobell Foundation
Wates Foundation

SPONSORS
BBC
Dom Perignon
Links of London
Pemberton Greenish
Smythson of Bond Street

BUSINESS BENEFACTORS & MEMBERS
Grey London
Hugo Boss
Lazard
Merrill Lynch
Vanity Fair

INDIVIDUAL SUPPORTERS

ICE-BREAKERS
Act IV
Anonymous
Ossi and Paul Burger
Mrs Helena Butler
Cynthia Corbett
Shantelle David
Charlotte & Nick Fraser
Mark & Rebecca Goldbart
Linda Grosse
Mr & Mrs Tim Harvey-Samuel
David Lanch
Colette & Peter Levy

Watcyn Lewis
David Marks
Nicola McFarland
Janet & Michael Orr
Pauline Pinder
Mr & Mrs William Poeton
The Really Useful Group
Lois Sieff OBE
Gail Steele
Nick & Louise Steidl

GROUND-BREAKERS
Anonymous
Moira Andreae
Jane Attias*
Elizabeth & Adam Bandeen
Philip Blackwell
Mrs D H Brett
Sindy & Jonathan Caplan
Mr & Mrs Gavin Casey
Carole & Neville Conrad
Clyde Cooper
Andrew & Amanda Cryer
Robyn M Durie
Hugo Eddis
Mrs Margaret Exley CBE
Robert & Sarah Fairbairn
Celeste & Peter Fenichel
Andrew & Jane Fenwick
Ginny Finegold
Wendy Fisher
Hugh & Henri Fitzwilliam-Lay
Joachim Fleury
Lydia & Manfred Gorvy
Richard & Marcia Grand*
Nick & Catherine Hanbury-Williams
Sam & Caroline Haubold
Nicholas Josefowitz
David P Kaskel & Christopher A Teano
Peter & Maria Kellner*
Mrs Joan Kingsley &
Mr Philip Kingsley
Mr & Mrs Pawel Kisielewski
Varian Ayers and Gary Knisely
Kathryn Ludlow
Emma Marsh
Duncan Matthews QC

Barbara Minto
Gavin & Ann Neath
Paul & Jill Ruddock
William & Hilary Russell
Jenny Sheridan
Anthony Simpson & Susan Boster
Brian D Smith
Carl & Martha Tack
Katherine & Michael Yates

BOUNDARY-BREAKERS
John and Annoushka Ayton
Katie Bradford
Tim Fosberry
Edna & Peter Goldstein
Reade and Elizabeth Griffith
Sue & Don Guiney
Rosanna Laurence
Jan and Michael Topham

MOVER-SHAKERS
Anonymous
Dianne & Michael Bienes*
Lois Cox
Cas & Philip Donald
John Garfield
Miles Morland

HISTORY-MAKERS
Jack & Linda Keenan*
Ian & Carol Sellars

MAJOR DONORS
Anonymous
Daniel & Joanna Friel
Lady Sainsbury of Turville
NoraLee & Jon Sedmak*

*Supporters of the American Friends of the Royal Court

FOR THE ROYAL COURT

Royal Court Theatre, Sloane Square, London SW1W 8AS
Tel: 020 7565 5050 Fax: 020 7565 5001
info@royalcourttheatre.com, www.royalcourttheatre.com

Artistic Director **Dominic Cooke**
Associate Directors **Ramin Gray*, Sacha Wares⁺**
Artistic Associate **Emily McLaughlin**
Associate Producer **Diane Borger**
Diversity Associate **Ola Animashawun***
Trainee Director (ITV Scheme) **Natalie Ibu‡**
Artistic Assistant **Rebecca Hanna-Grindall**

Literary Manager **Ruth Little**
Literary Associate **Terry Johnson***
Pearson Playwright **Daniel Jackson†**
Literary Assistant **Nicola Wass**

Associate Director International **Elyse Dodgson**
International Administrator **Chris James**
International Assistant **William Drew**

YWP Manager **Nina Lyndon**
Outreach Worker **Lucy Dunkerley**
Writers' Tutor **Leo Butler***

Casting Director **Amy Ball**
Casting Assistant **Lotte Hines**

Head of Production **Paul Handley**
JTU Production Manager **Sue Bird**
Production Assistant **Sarah Davies**
Head of Lighting **Matt Drury**
Lighting Deputy **Nicki Brown**
Lighting Assistants **Stephen Andrews, Katie Pitt**
Lighting Board Operator **Joe Hicks**
Head of Stage **Steven Stickler**
Stage Deputy **Duncan Russell**
Stage Chargehand **Lee Crimmen**
Chargehand Carpenter **Richard Martin**
Head of Sound **Ian Dickinson**
Sound Deputy **David McSeveney**
Head of Costume **Iona Kenrick**
Costume Deputy **Jackie Orton**
Wardrobe Assistant **Pam Anson**

Executive Director **Kate Horton**
Head of Finance and Administration **Helen Perryer**
Senior Finance and Administration Officer **Martin Wheeler**
Finance Officer **Rachel Harrison***
Finance and Administration Assistant **Tessa Rivers**

Head of Communications **Kym Bartlett**
Marketing Manager **Becky Wootton**
Press Officer **Stephen Pidcock**
Audience Development Officer **Gemma Frayne**

Sales Manager **Kevin West**
Deputy Sales Manager **Daniel Alicandro**
Box Office Sales Assistants **Fiona Clift, Shane Hough, Ciara O'Toole**

Head of Development **Jenny Mercer**
Development Manager **Hannah Clifford**
Development Assistant **Lucy James**

Theatre Manager **Bobbie Stokes**
Front of House Manager **Claire Simpson**
Deputy Theatre Manager **Daniel O'Neill**
Duty Managers **Stuart Grey*, Rebecca Hanna-Grindall***
Bar and Food Manager **Darren Elliott**
Deputy Bar and Food Manager **Paul Carstairs**
Bookshop Manager **Simon David**
Assistant Bookshop Manager **Edin Suljic***
Bookshop Assistant **Emily Lucienne**
Building Maintenance Administrator **Jon Hunter**
Stage Door/Reception **Simon David*, Paul Lovegrove, Tyrone Lucas**

Thanks to all of our box office assistants, ushers and bar staff.

+ Sacha Wares' post is supported by the BBC through the Gerald Chapman Fund.

‡ The post of Trainee Director is supported by ITV under the ITV Theatre Director Scheme.

† This theatre has the support of the Pearson Playwrights' scheme, sponsored the Peggy Ramsay Foundation.

* Part-time.

ENGLISH STAGE COMPANY

President
Sir John Mortimer CBE QC

Vice President
Dame Joan Plowright CBE

Honorary Council
Sir Richard Eyre CBE
Alan Grieve CBE
Martin Paisner CBE

Council
Chairman **Anthony Burton**
Vice Chairman **Graham Devlin**

Members
Jennette Arnold
Judy Daish
Sir David Green KCMG
Joyce Hytner OBE
Stephen Jeffreys
Phyllida Lloyd
James Midgley
Sophie Okonedo
Alan Rickman
Anita Scott
Katharine Viner
Stewart Wood

Now or Later

Be bloody, or be nothing

Hamlet

Characters

John, *twenty, white*
Matt, *twenty, white*
Marc, *thirties, Jewish*
Jessica, *early fifties, white*
Tracy, *forties, black*
John Sr, *mid-fifties, white*

A note on the design

During the play characters watch television and look at a computer screen. At no time should these images be visible to the audience.

My feeling is that the play will be most effective with a spartan design in all areas.

Late night, election day. A hotel room in a Southern state.

John *reads.* **Matt** *is at his laptop. A knock.* **John** *hides in the closet.*

Marc   Is John around?

Matt   He went to smoke.

Marc   You expect him back?

Matt   Um . . . he said he might make some phone calls.

Marc   Did he say where he went?

Matt   Um . . .

Marc   Like he went to the stairwell or he went out somewhere?

Matt   I'm not sure.

Pause.

All right, do me a favor, what's his cell so I can call him?

Matt   I think.

I think he left his phone actually.

Marc   He went to make some phone calls and he left his phone.

All right. When he gets back please have him call me. Because I need to speak to him again about the pictures.

Marc *goes.*

John   I want this to be over!

Matt   Sorry. I thought, what if your phone rings from the closet –

John   I already told him I'm not putting out a statement, what does he want? Do a search, see if there's anything new.

Let's go Florida! Ohio! Let's get this thing over with already!

Matt   It doesn't seem like it's been picked up. It's still just on those blogs.

John   What would the story be? 'Candidate's Son Attends Crazy College Party'?

Matt   Maybe they're thinking this could become a big deal.

John   How? It would be one thing if I was, like, a member of the senior staff or a future cabinet member, then I could see how this might turn into something. But who cares about my going to some ridiculous party, how could that impact my father? I'm a college student, I did what I'm supposed to do on a Friday night, I got hammered and acted like an idiot.

Matt   Remember when I took that class on the modern presidency? One of the big things was how quickly Republicans defined the Democrats in '92, as soon as the election was over – gays in the military, health care. The mid-term elections were a disaster, Republicans controlled the narrative, and that was it, Contract With America, the end of all hope for progressive legislation for over a decade. The lesson was, stay in control of your narrative, if you let the other guys define you –

John   I don't understand, what could anyone say about these pictures that would in any way affect or define my father's narrative? You're talking about how in '92 the Republicans defined the Democrats based on issues, based on the President's and the party's policy proposals.

Matt   Right . . . but that was, like – early nineties, no internet, no viral spread of this whole kind of insubstantial, like – amorphous, gossipy personal stuff that can disproportionately impact the discourse – some stupid thing that starts on a blog and a week later is on the front pages –

John   I understand what you're saying, but not how it applies. We were being jackasses at an off-campus party – it's not like we revealed anything about my father, or state secrets or something. What's the story?

Matt   Yeah . . .

Marc (*offstage*)   Hey, John, it's Marc, you have a minute?

Hey, buddy. Listen, there's been some more discussion upstairs about these pictures. I know what you said before about your privacy, but we wanted to ask you again if it's all right if we just put out a really under-the-radar statement that says that you regret your choice of costume. Is that cool with you?

John   Marc, what's everyone so nervous about?

Marc   We're just being cautious. It looks like a good night for us, we want to make sure everything's taken care of.

John   What's there to take care of? This is on three blogs no one's ever heard of. The pictures are blurry, you can barely see anything.

Marc   Let me just read it to you –

John   You know my dad's policy is that I have say over any aspect of the campaign that has to do with me –

Marc   That's why we're checking with you –

John   So first I want to know, what's everyone so worried about? You're being really vague.

Pause.

Marc   There's concern that some news organizations who are hostile to your dad might try to use this story to discredit him.

John   Discredit him how?

Marc   Ivy League school, President-elect's son goes to a Halloween party dressed up as Muhammad, his friend dressed up like Pastor Bob –

John   I told you, it wasn't a Halloween party – that makes me like some arrogant xenophobe –

Marc   I know what you told me – but in terms of us, how we handle this, we think it's better if we just say it's a Halloween party –

John   Wait – this is me, this isn't something for you to say any way at all.

Marc   If you – I understand that. What I meant was, if you feel like – we're just trying to come up with a way to deflect this in case –

John   What you mean is, you've all already decided that in fact I don't have a choice about this, and you're going to put out a statement from me.

Marc   If you – yes, we want to put out a really simple, basic statement that will put this thing to bed, if you'll agree to it.

John   I don't understand what would wake it up.

Marc   It's woken up, John. No disrespect, but – you have anti-Muslim stuff, anti-Christian, elitism – obviously we don't know what will happen, but we're planning for the worst.

John   Which is . . .

Marc   You're a Democrat, right?

John   It makes me cringe to admit it, but – yeah.

Marc   Well, apart from this thing taking on a life of its own and becoming a distraction because of the nature of the internet – we think whoever put these pictures out there has an agenda. Meaning, this is not some prank, this is a high-up, Republican Party dirty trick to sabotage your dad, to get in the way of his first few days of press – which are really important in terms of laying the foundation to get future legislation passed.

John   How could the Republican Party – how could they use this to further their agenda? 'The President's son went to a party, therefore we refuse to pass the President's economic stimulus package'?

Marc   It's more than a party. There's a pretty big backstory to all this, right?

John   To what?

Marc   To your feelings about Muslims.

John   Uh . . . not that I'm aware of.

Marc Well – I don't know the whole story, but I guess you wrote an anti-Muslim editorial for your school paper in September –

John Anti-Muslim? No. What happened was, cartoons depicting Muhammad were put up around campus anonymously and the Muslim Student Association tried to use that to change the university's freedom-of-speech policy, so whoever did it could be expelled. I wrote an op-ed defending the school's current policy – I didn't defend the content of the cartoons, that was beside the point. I just focused on the right to freedom of expression, regardless of whether people find the expression offensive or not. A couple of blogs linked to it, my mom called and asked me to not write any more op-eds till after the election – and that was it. The end.

Marc Somebody upstairs found an editorial responding to your editorial that made it seem like a lot of the Muslim students thought that what you wrote was anti-Muslim.

John The Muslim Student Association wanted to consider the cartoons hate speech, they argued that they would lead directly to violence against Muslims. I wrote that a link like that couldn't be proven and so shouldn't be used to curtail or redefine freedom of speech – which some people took as my saying that I advocated violence against Muslims, since I was supporting the kind of speech that they said causes it.

Marc Well, these pictures are out there, there's a record of you and this Muslim controversy – you know what the press is like, I mean –

John It's an Ivy League kerfuffle, I don't see how it could become more than that. Of all the possible things to write about tomorrow . . .

Is there something you're not telling me?

Pause.

Marc The thing is – I think this has reached a point where we were coming to you out of respect, but – the decision's already been made to put out an apology.

John 'Already been made.' Who made that decision? What are you not telling me?

Pause.

Does my father know about this?

Marc I don't have access to your father.

John Well, tell whoever is making this decision about me and my words that this is not their decision to make.

Marc *goes.*

John What are they so paranoid about? This is like a campaign-induced psychosis – Talking-Heads' Disease! Pundit's Fever!

Who do you think put these pictures out there? 'Quick, put down the bong, get the camera, he's persecuting Muslims!'

Matt It's weird he couldn't really say what they think might happen.

John Because on some latent level they realize that nothing *will* happen, they're just being pathologically cautious. He's totally fucking my mother, by the way. They kept sharing looks all through dinner.

Matt In front of your dad?

John He probably didn't even notice. I swear he's asexual – except for when he's making love to the clam dip.

Why do I keep thinking Robbie's going to call? What is wrong with me?

Matt It's only been a month . . .

John No more thinking he'll call. From this moment forth.

I wonder if my dad is orchestrating this whole 'put out a statement' thing from behind the scenes.

Matt Why would he do that?

John Because he's scared of facing me himself and having to admit that he's trying to pressure me into doing something.

When I got wasted and flipped my Jeep over in high school we made this contract in therapy where he agreed that I could be my own person, and that I'd never have to participate in anything political that I didn't want to ever again – and he's really stuck to that. He hasn't asked me to do a single thing this campaign, he just wanted me to be at the convention and here on election night. He even told me I could come out of the closet if I wanted to.

Matt   That's really cool.

John   Of course he knew I wouldn't do it, he knows I want to keep my privacy. I remember, though, in therapy, after we made the agreement, Dr Green warned me – if my dad ran for President I would have to be ready to stand up for myself, because I'd probably start feeling pressure again. That's what I'm worried about – today it's, 'Apologize for dressing up as Muhammad,' but next week it's something like, 'Don't take that class, the professor is critical of Israel, if it gets out it'll hurt us with the Jews.'

Matt   You think they would go that far?

John   These people hold focus groups on what color ties to wear! They take polls on what part of the country to vacation in! The re-election campaign begins tonight.

If he wants me to apologize he should have the balls to come down here and tell me himself. He's sending down surrogates like it's international diplomacy. – Colorado.

Matt   Colorado?

Jessica *enters.*

Jessica   Did you see? – we won Colorado.

John   How did you get in?

Jessica   The door was open.

John   Still you don't knock?

Jessica   The door was open!

John   I can't believe he left the door open!

Jessica   Whatever, I'm in. Who's this?

John   This is my good friend Matt, from school.

Jessica   Hello, Matt, nice to meet you. Are you a fellow psych major?

Matt   Political science.

Jessica   Oh! Maybe a future intern.

John   Not quite. Matt wants to do community organizing.

Jessica   Oh!

Matt   My mom was really active in the community, that's the tradition I come from.

Jessica   That's wonderful . . . I've been amazed at how many grassroots volunteers we have working for us, it's been so inspiring to see that kind of passion.

John   That's not what he means by community organizing.

Matt   It's similar in a way. Trying to get marginalized people to work together to effect change –

John   One of Matt's first memories is of his mom at a rally chanting 'No blood for oil!' before the first Iraq War.

Jessica   Really. John never lets us forget that one of his first memories is of being posed for a campaign photo for my husband's Senate re-election.

John   One of? It's *the* first – I had to pee so badly and they wouldn't let me! Who doesn't let a three-year-old pee?

Pause.

Matt   I voted for your husband today!

John   Like me, against his better judgment.

Jessica   Thank you, we appreciate your vote.

It's very nice to meet you.

Matt *goes.*

Jessica Is that Pastor Bob?

John You could tell?

So you know all about this. Mom, this is ridiculous.

Jessica Did it not occur to you that something like this might happen if you went out on Halloween dressed as Muhammad?

John It wasn't Halloween – who is spreading that? That makes me come off as some kind of nihilistic transgressive hipster pervert!

Jessica As opposed to . . .

John Okay: a couple weekends ago, this girl from my twentieth-century lit class threw a naked party –

Jessica A *naked* party?

John They didn't have naked parties when you were in school?

Jessica Tell me what one is and I'll tell you if we had them.

John There's a series of rooms, and the further you go into the rooms the less and less clothing people are wearing, until you get to the final room and everyone is naked.

Pause.

Jessica We didn't have those.

John Okay, so, this girl – this, like, pro-sex feminist comp-lit major – the day of the party, we're in class, and out of nowhere she starts to cry. The professor asks her what's wrong and she starts going off on the cartoons – how she can't stop thinking about them, how they're actually *worse* than physical violence, because they dehumanize Muslim people, which is the precondition for future violence against Muslim people to take place with impunity. And half the class is like nodding along and making little sounds of support – and most of these people are going to the naked party! They see no contradiction between going to the naked party and their conspicuous silence about the fundamentalist culture the cartoons were critiquing, a culture that does not allow women to bare their forearms, let alone attend 'naked' parties. So I speak up and try to point out that some of the cartoons were in fact taking aim at the limits on female sexual expression in Islamic society and do we really want to prohibit speech that critiques misogyny in the Islamic world, which would be one result of the Muslim Student Association's successfully arguing that these cartoons constitute hate speech. The naked-party girl gets *hysterical* and tells me I'm a 'cultural imperialist', then this other girl starts shouting that Islamic women may choose to live in their culture but that they can't choose whether or not to get blown up by our bombs, which she says with a little smile on her face like she's saying my dad's going to be the next one to drop them and I'm the son of a murderer – then this kid who is *obsessed* with theory, every book we read he starts out the discussion by quoting theory and never talks about the book, he says that women get date-raped on campus all the time and if I care so much about the oppression of women why don't I write op-eds about them, why do I only care about the oppression of women if they're Islamic – which the class seems to think is so totally devastating that a few of them break into applause. At this point I give up. Fine.

Later that night, a spur-of-the-moment thing, Matt and I decided to dress up as Pastor Bob and Muhammad and crash the party, and tell people they were going to burn in hell.

Pause.

Jessica Why don't we start by having a cup of tea? Would you like one?

John Start what?

Jessica Start talking about this.

John What's there to talk about, Mom?

Jessica Cup of tea?

John   How about a beer?

Jessica   Good idea, maybe I'll have one too –

John   Don't!

Jessica   What?

John   If you get them from the minibar they'll be automatically charged to the room.

Jessica   So?

John   So, I don't think the campaign should be paying for us to have fifteen-dollar beers.

Jessica   What are you talking about?

John   People don't donate their money to a campaign so the candidate's son can drink beer for free. We'll order from room service and pay with cash.

Jessica   John, half the country is probably drunk tonight, I'm sure they wouldn't mind your having a beer.

We'll leave a nice tip for the maid to make up for it, how about that?

John   I'm not drinking it.

Pause.

Jessica   So what's going on, what happened with Robbie?

John   What – is my room bugged or something? How do you know about Robbie?

Jessica   At the convention you told us that Robbie would be with you on election night.

Pause.

John   We broke up, I don't want to talk about it.

Jessica   What happened?

You're my son, I want to know!

John   He didn't want to be monogamous anymore.

Which was a shock to me since, when we fell in love, he said a big part of why he fell in love with me was that I wanted a monogamous relationship. Which not a lot of gay guys do.

Jessica   They don't?

John   No. Especially not at Ivy League universities, where queer-theory professors teach that gay people who want monogamous relationships have self-loathingly internalized the value system of an oppressive patriarchal heteronormative culture.

I might as well have a Scarlet M pinned to my chest.

Jessica   I don't know what to say. I thought things had changed in the gay world.

John   Well, it doesn't help that politicians continue to deny gay people the right to marry, which sends a pretty clear signal. Why try to have something that society says you don't deserve and won't get?

Pause.

Jessica   Is Matt . . . ?

John   Say the word, say it, I know you can!

Jessica   Gay, gay! I can say it!

John   He's straight.

Jessica   He seemed a little gay.

John   He's a socialist.

Anyway, you obviously want to talk about the pictures.

Jessica   The pictures –

John   What is John's position?

Pause.

Jessica   Your father doesn't know yet.

John   He doesn't?

Jessica   I think if he knew, he'd be very upset. Don't you?

Pause.

John   Why would he be upset? I'm not an envoy to Pakistan, I'm not brokering peace in the Middle East –

Jessica   You read the news – you know what happened with the cartoons in Denmark, and when they tried to give the knighthood in England –

John   But I'm not a newspaper cartoonist, I didn't write a novel – I'm a college student, I went to a party. Mom, I won't be forced into becoming a media figure over three blurry pictures just because some hyperbolic political advisor needs to cover his ass. I want a normal life! I want to not live in a bubble of insanity –

Jessica   No one's going to take away your autonomy – what you do is up to you. But from one adult to another – I think you have to seriously consider making an apology.

John   Well, I have considered it. I don't see the need.

Pause.

Jessica   You've thought about what could happen –

John   Hypothetical. Nothing is happening.

Jessica   What if it does?

John   Then we'll deal with it then.

Pause.

Jessica   Tracy was just asking about you.

John   She was?

Jessica   She asked me if you were going to make a trip upstairs at any point. I told her, don't hold your breath.

John   She and I had such a good time at the convention.

Jessica   She's trying to bring a little fun to the proceedings – without much success. Everyone is so serious. Your grandfather's the worst of the bunch – he's become convinced that the stage decorations are 'effeminate', he wants your father to have them removed.

John (*texting*)   That'll inspire the crowd.

Jessica   He has his whole thing about how Democrats get tagged as soft.

John   He's just jealous he never got to be President.

Jessica   Your father's been pretending to take his advice the whole campaign, you'd think on election night he could tell him to fuck off. But no, there he is, earnestly listening as Grandpa tells him that the sentences in his speech are too long.

John   Actually, Grandpa has a point there.

Pause.

Jessica   . . . *Adolescence and Developmental Breakdown.* Some light reading?

John   It's good.

Jessica   Is this a book for school or . . . for yourself?

John   Mom, don't worry!

Jessica   I'm not worried –

John   This is what I want to do with my life, I'm going to be reading books like this –

Jessica   I'm just – okay. They still use words like 'breakdown'? That sounds so antiquated.

John   It's a collection of papers from the seventies and eighties, before the pharmaceutical companies and shrinks convinced everyone that the only thing wrong with America is the brain chemistry of its citizens. I found it in this used bookstore, it looked familiar, and then I remembered that Dr Green had a copy of it in his office.

Jessica   You remembered it from all those years ago? Wow. Do you stay in touch with Dr Green?

John   No, it's not really allowed.

Jessica   He really changed your life, didn't he?

John   He didn't just change my life, he saved it. I wanted to die.

Pause.

Jessica   I remember.

Matt *enters.*

Matt   You guys watching? I just heard someone in the hall say they called Ohio!

Jessica   We got it?

Fantastic. Maybe now people will start having a good time. Wish me luck!

She goes.

Matt   Got your text. You think your dad knows about the pictures?

John   No doubt. It's just like him: avoid conflict, stay above the fray, keep your hands clean – then get your way. She was definitely treading lightly, though. She looked at what I was reading and it was like an alarm started ringing in her head – I think they're scared I'll go off the rails again if they do something without my approval. I wonder what their next tactic will be. Maybe John himself will make an appearance.

Matt   So you really think they have this whole strategy –

John   Everything they do is strategic. Giving birth to me was strategic. Even when they finally took me to therapy in high school – they only did it because you can't get elected President if your son kills himself. Looking back – there were so many signs I was fucked up, long before I flipped my Jeep. But they didn't notice or care until the accident – which of course was all over the news.

Matt   I'm sure they also really love you.

John   In the context of my dad's political career. They're
textbook narcissists. Their entire lives have been organised
around my dad becoming President. He's probably just freaking
out that these pictures are going to stain his big moment. It's
so crazy! You're always thinking tactically, so you spend all
your time worrying that every fart is going to turn into a shit
storm. You wouldn't even know I was Muhammad if I hadn't
written 'Muhammad' on my T-shirt. My turban is made of
two pillowcases. You're wearing a Hawaiian shirt with a pillow
underneath and holding a copy of Pastor Bob's book. How
could they be worried? Seriously – let's say you had to make
the case – what would you argue?

Matt   About this becoming an issue?

John   What ramifications are they so worried about? Put
yourself in my dad's mindset. One of your eighteen senior
advisors brings you over to his iBook and you see three out-
of-focus pictures from a college party . . . What goes through
your mind?

Matt   Well – maybe it's more than just politics they're
worried about.

John   Like what?

Matt   Like – remember a few years ago, there was that radio
talk-show host, I forget where – he was liberal, but as a kind
of test he said on-air something like, 'All Muslim Americans
should be forced to wear armbands so we can recognize them
in public.' He had literally hundreds and hundreds of calls of
support come in to the station, people saying they agreed with
him.

John   Disgusting.

Matt   That's what I mean. There's a lot of ugliness out there
toward Muslims, so maybe they're looking at the pictures and
they're really worried about what kind of impact it could have –
if people think you're anti-Muslim.

John   But if I'd said something discriminatory like that, from
a public platform, I'd totally understand the need to apologize.

Matt   You don't think people could see it as similar?

John   Wearing a Muhammad costume at a private party and publicly advocating massive civil rights violations against all Muslims?

Matt   I don't know if anything is really private anymore, though. And the religion thing is a really tough one. For us, religion is a kind of escape from society, but in the Muslim world, it's like religion brings all these different facets of life together, so it's a lot bigger deal to make fun of it.

John   What do you mean?

Matt   The Muslim world is angry about a lot of things, right? American foreign and economic policy, Israel and Palestine, their own governments being in bed with us . . . for us, no matter how pious our leaders are, church and state are separate, so making fun of religion has a different connotation. But over there it's all a lot closer together – so I think religious worship represents more than just devotion to God, it's also a way of organizing against Western policies and values. For an American, a non-Muslim, to make fun of Muhammad – it's like you're saying that their entire society and their feelings about oppression aren't legitimate.

John   Right . . .

Matt   I'm not disagreeing with you – I think freedom of expression is really important, I mean, I went to the party, I'm with you about our school's speech policy – but that was just school. If the pictures spread . . .

Pause.

Tracy (*offstage, knocks*)   What's going on in there? Is there a party going on in there?

John   Tracy!

Tracy   Tell me I found the party – please!

John   I wish. Is it bad up there?

Tracy   I just want to celebrate! Look, we're gonna win this thing because we were the biggest bunch of neurotic worriers you could ever hope to assemble in one campaign, and trust me, I worry with the best of them – but there is a time to stop worrying and start partying!

She takes beer from the minibar.

I don't know you, are you the boyfriend?

John   This is my friend Matt.

Matt   You spoke in my modern presidency class.

Tracy   You're not the boyfriend?

John   It's a long story.

Tracy   I want to hear it, what happened?

John   Typical gay breakup.

Tracy   He cheated? You cheated?

John   I didn't cheat – I would never cheat!

Tracy   They all say that till they do. How many gay male friends do I have, every single one of them –

John   Not me.

Tracy   So you caught him – was it ugly?

John   No, it was theoretical – he wanted to have sex with other people, he tried to convince me that it would keep things 'fresh' for us, and that I'd like it too, that it's important for gay people to 'keep transgression alive' –

Tracy   You got the full propaganda package.

John   Oh yeah – the wonderful world of non-monogamy, as only an Ivy Leaguer can rationalize it.

Tracy   And you wouldn't go along with it. You stood up to that creep. You go!

John   I wish I was that heroic. More like curled up in a fetal position clinging to myself to stop from shaking while he's saying, 'I don't *understand*, I still *love* you.'

Tracy   You should go straight, I'm telling you. All my gay friends now, I tell them, these ex-gays are onto something. They figured something out!

John   So you don't have anyone to set me up with?

Tracy   Oh Lord. I know a lot of guys who'd like to be set up with you – you, I don't think, would feel the same about them.

John   Old?

Tracy   You're like the most handsome young man! You don't read what they write about you on the gay message boards?

John   No – is it good?

Tracy   Even the lesbians want your ass! Come on. You know you're hot!

John   A lot of good it did me with Robbie.

Tracy   You have to forget him – and that's it. In fact we should stop talking about this, it's no way to have a party, talking about exes.

John   So you really think this is over, huh? My dad won?

Tracy   Any minute they'll call Florida, your dad'll get the phone call, he'll check his hair in the mirror, and then he'll be right outside that window telling the world that sanity is back in the White House.

John   There's no alternative scenario where he can still lose?

Tracy   No. But, you know, I never thought there was an alternative scenario. The only way you could've thought we'd lose this one is if you think people are insane. I think people can be stupid but I don't think they're insane, and I thought this time they were gonna figure it out. What's scary to me is, even when it's an obvious choice, how many millions of people still go the other way.

Matt   It's such great news. I remember when you spoke in my class – I felt so pessimistic. You talked about the Democratic Party's shift to the center in the nineties and how even that

wasn't enough to win a majority of the popular vote, in either
election, how they might not have won at all had there not
been a third-party candidate. You said we had to admit that
the U.S. is fundamentally a conservative country and just get
used to it.

Tracy   I'd amend that a little today. It is true about America –
you poll people on individual issues, and a huge majority are
progressive on the issues – and then they end up voting
Republican! It's this amazing thing, we want big changes, but
in a very slow way. So somehow when you run a campaign you
have to work with that contradiction, seem like you're gonna
do a lot and not much at the same time.

But this time I felt like things shifted just a little. There was an
anger, an outrage in the country I hadn't seen before. I mean,
you can be smarty-pants about it and say we ran a centrist
campaign – and we did in many ways – but it was not a
nineties centrist campaign, it was not us trying to mimic the
Republicans without alienating our base. We were drawing real
distinctions and speaking with passion about our beliefs. We still
triangulated, but the left side of that triangle got just a little
bigger, a little stronger, and those other two sides shrunk a little.

Matt   Do you think Democrats will be able to govern from
the center-left, or will the Republicans push them to the right
like they did in the nineties?

Tracy   Really, will the Democrats let themselves be pushed?
But I don't want to think about that tonight – it's too
depressing. Governing is a whole different thing.

John   Also, my dad's actually a lot more conservative than
he's portrayed himself in the campaign.

Tracy   Oh, I don't think so. I have to say, I've been around a
lot of politicians, I think your dad really believes what he says.
To be elected as a Democrat in the South in the eighties and
nineties, there were some things you had to be on the right
about. That's where I grew up, I remember. But times change,
the people evolve – and as of tonight he's not a regional
politician anymore.

John   But I remember him around the dinner table – I think
he really does believe a lot of that stuff. We used to go fishing
when I was little, and on the drive out he'd talk about politics –
I remember him talking to me about liberal interest groups
and how they were ruining the Democratic Party, how
Democrats in the northeast didn't understand how deeply the
South valued life, the right to bear arms, traditional values. He
was really passionate about it – I don't think it was just politics
when he voted for the Defense of Marriage Act. He voted for
welfare reform, against affirmative action, his foreign policy
record is way to the right –

Tracy   We all carry things from where we're from. We learn,
we realize we made mistakes when we were younger . . . And
on a lot of things, I think on health care, the environment, the
economy, he was much more to the left than his Senate voting
record. Now he has a chance to be himself on those issues,
the times have caught up with him, and on other issues, like
foreign policy, some social issues, he's caught up with the times.
You couldn't run on universal health care and win eight years
ago. You couldn't run on climate change.

John   Don't hold your breath on foreign policy. I'm convinced
of that – if it takes blowing up the Middle East to stay in
power, he will, no matter what his campaign rhetoric is.

Tracy   Well . . . we'll see. Speaking of foreign policy –
Muhammad! In the house! And Pastor Bob!

John   Oh God!

Tracy   Unbelievable. I'm definitely inviting you two to my
next party.

John   My mom is freaking out about this.

Tracy   I'm freaking out too.

Pause.

John   You are?

Tracy   Those people go crazy over stuff like this! Look,
I don't get Islam, I don't pretend to, but what I do know is,

this stuff gets real bad real fast. That's why I think, who knows what they'll do whether you apologize or not, but you might as well just apologize so you can say you did your part, and if they start rioting and killing people, that's their own doing.

John   But – you can't argue that someone's speech is – if I don't apologize and they kill people or – not that that would ever happen, but –

Tracy   I wouldn't be so sure of that. I bet some imam in Iran or Syria issues a fatwa – if just for the PR.

John   That's – really? No –

Tracy   This is serious stuff, disrespecting their prophet is against their law! That's why I think you should just apologize, get it over with. I'm not saying they're right – I mean, I come from oppressed people that white people did a lot of bad shit to, and to me Islam could not be more incomprehensible – it is beyond my brain. But I have eyes. I can see it, I see what they do. And when they feel disrespected you do not wanna mess with them!

John   But nothing's – I mean – you don't think you're exaggerating what –

Tracy   No. I think this is big. I'm looking at you, I don't think this has sunk in yet.

Pause.

John   Matt was saying something before you came in . . .

Tracy   What were you saying?

Pause.

Matt   Just – like, my mom raised me to be an atheist, because she thought religion made people accept their lot instead of fight to improve it.

Tracy   Uh-huh?

Matt   Which I think is true. In America, religious people – they don't see their religion as having a political component.

Religion is not a way into the political sphere, it's a safe haven from it.

Tracy   Really? This is coming from Pastor Bob himself?

Matt   Oh, definitely the Christian right, the evangelicals, they – but they focus mostly on social policy. What I mean is, in the Muslim world religion has a much broader function, it's a way for people to feel they have agency, to respond actively to globalization and war. If you mock their religion, you're mocking what they feel across the board. Here the religious is linked to the political, but there the religious *is* the political.

Tracy   I see. It's true, they don't have the separation and the symbolic space for speech that comes from that. That's why a word or an image is like an action to them.

John   But – okay, for them the religious is the political. But the religious is also the religious.

Tracy   Which means what?

John   Which means – I totally agree that the Muslim world has grievances against the West that are valid – not just valid but correct, a lot of them – but even so, even if their religious fundamentalism has deeper political components, it's still also religious fundamentalism. It's still a literalist reading of the Qu'ran, which is used to justify the oppression, and worse, of gay people, women, non-believers – the West didn't invent sharia law. And there are millions of moderate people in these countries who object to American policy without also believing in jihad.

Tracy   So what's your point?

John   For Muslims who read the Qu'ran literally, even if America were a totally benevolent and selfless country in its interactions with Islamic countries, factions in these countries would still be advocating jihad. So, if the argument is that I should apologize to Muslims because in making fun of Muhammad I'm also, to them, making fun of their legitimate grievances – I'm just saying that those grievances are not the whole story, Islam has hatred and intolerance in it that have nothing to do with Western oppression. It makes an apology a lot more complex, because my apology can be interpreted by them as an acknowledgment that their value system is legitimate – and if I submit to it then I'm betraying all those people who are oppressed by that system –

Tracy   You're making it too complicated. What Matt's saying – he's just saying you can't hold another culture to the standards you hold your own culture to. You have to compromise and see things their way a little, you have to acknowledge and respect that their culture is different than yours.

John   But – at a certain level there really is just one standard, whatever the cultural differences. If a fundamentalist Muslim tries to hang me for being gay – how do I compromise with that?

Tracy   (*laughs*)   Oh, come on! No one is trying to kill you for being a gay boy!

John   Two seconds ago you were talking about a fatwa!

Tracy   John!

John   I'm serious! What should I say? 'Please don't hang me, but feel free to chop off the hand I jerk off with'? That might be a compromise to them – it's not to me!

Tracy   You know that's a diversionary argument. This is just about realizing that for people in this culture, Muhammad is their prophet, they feel a certain way about him, you make fun of him and it's a big deal to them. The logical thing to do is say you're sorry.

John   But the fact that their culture is homophobic is a big deal to me, and I don't walk up to women in traditional dress and say, 'Take off your hijab, the symbols of your religion are offensive to me as a gay man.' They're allowed to think I'm going to hell for being gay, I'm allowed to think their religion is ridiculous!

Tracy   You're putting them on a level playing field with yourself and that is not the case. You are more sophisticated than they are, you know you're not going to hell no matter what they believe. But they don't know you're just making a harmless joke about their prophet, they can't see things that way. Why can't you see how they see you?

John   I can see how they see me! That's the problem – they need to see me differently – as having a right to my opinion!

Tracy   And you need to see them differently, the way Matt is talking about.

John   The two things are not equal, Tracy! Having a right to not be killed for an opinion is reasonable, having a right to not have anyone ever say anything bad about your religion is not reasonable!

Tracy   Come on, this is a right-wing thing, to always talk about being killed by these people.

John   Then why did you bring up a fatwa?

Tracy   You know, you really are like your dad. I don't mean that in a bad way, it's just funny to see.

John   How am I like him?

Tracy   You both have to be right!

John   I don't *have* to be right, but if I think I *am* right I'm not going to say I'm *wrong* –

Tracy   That was the hardest thing to get him to do in those debates, not put forward this air that he is always right all the time.

John   How am I putting forward an air?

Tracy   Matt, back me up on this one –

Matt   They just called Florida.

They watch TV.

Tracy   That's right . . .

John   Maybe now everyone will stop freaking out about the pictures.

Tracy *gets a text.*

Tracy   Video from the party is online.

We'd been hearing this might happen.

She goes.

John   See if you can find it.

Matt   I bet I know what it is. Do you remember the
dominatrix?

Pause.

The girl who was dressed up like one? She kept waving around
this huge dildo all night . . . ?

At one point you grabbed it from her and sort of − held it
against me and went down on it. For thirty seconds maybe.
A lot of people were around cheering, I remember seeing
some phones up in the air −

John   Find it.

Matt   Here − 'anonymously from a PhD student in the
Islamic Studies program' − 'released now so as not to be
accused of attempting to impact election results' −

John   I can't watch this.

Matt   'An example of virulent anti-Muslim sentiment on
campus and its tacit acceptance by the university community' −
'more traditional attempts to raise awareness have not had an
impact' −

John   Play it.

They watch. Pause.

Marc (*offstage, knocks*)   Hey, it's Marc.

John   Hi.

Marc   Hey. They asked me to come down here.

John   Why?

Marc   To make sure you guys don't go anywhere.

Pause.

John   What's happening?

Marc   They're going war room on this. It's not up for debate anymore.

John   Excuse me?

I asked you a question. Answer the question, don't be flip with me – is that clear?

Pause.

Marc   They want you to do a sit-down with an outside journalist, they think it's gone too far for just a statement. They're also working backchannel with some Muslim-American groups about what else you should do. One of the things is for you to meet with the Muslim student group and commit to addressing anti-Muslim hatred on campus.

John   Who is 'they', who is making these decisions – ?

Tracy (*offstage*)   Marc, come out here a minute.

Marc *exits.*

John   I know what this is about. This is about they have to show that the President's powerful. It's what you said, it's about the narrative. If the guy can't control his own son, how can he control the Congress? If he has no authority over his own family, how can he have authority as Commander-in-Chief? My dad doesn't give a fuck about Muslims – he's been wiping the Pentagon's ass from the day he got to Congress –

Tracy *enters.*

Tracy   Hey –

John   My dad knows.

Tracy   Yes.

John   What's happening?

Tracy   Who knows, now there's a debate, some people don't think we should start off a new Democratic administration by 'apologizing to Islamic extremists'.

John   Grandpa.

Tracy   Not only him. I just came to give you a heads-up – your dad's on his way down.

Tracy *goes.*

John   See? It's all about what makes them look the most powerful, it's all they care about.

Matt   Should I go?

John   No, I want you to stay.

Matt   Your dad won't want me here.

John   Go in the closet.

Matt   The closet? Won't Secret Service, like, sweep the room?

John   They stay outside, go.

Matt *goes in the closet.* **John Sr** *enters.*

John   Was the door open?

John Sr   They gave me a key. We don't have a lot of time to discuss this. Have a seat.

John *sits.*

John Sr   Before we get to the situation – your mother told me what happened with Robbie. I'm sorry you boys broke up.

John   Thanks.

John Sr   If I remember correctly, in your counseling with Dr Green, you and he talked a lot about how important it was for you to feel that you could have a loving relationship some day. I know this meant a lot to you.

Pause.

Now these pictures. Can you explain to me the intent behind all this?

John   This very left-wing girl threw a party, it had a sexual theme, and I thought it was a contradiction because she also supported this Muslim student group that wanted to change the university's freedom-of-speech policy. So I thought it would be a funny way of pointing out the contradiction between her throwing this libertine party and her support for a group that was trying to stifle freedom of expression, including expression critical of Islam's regressive views on female sexuality.

John Sr   I was shown the editorial you wrote. Obviously this is a highly charged issue on campus. I need to understand how this will be seen now. Explain to me the context.

John   The context is – these cartoons that made fun of Muhammad went up at school one night, anonymously, and as a result, the school's freedom-of-speech policy came under attack. Muslim students talked about the need for respect, without extending that respect, I felt, to people they may not agree with, who express things they don't like.

John Sr   So you're saying that your intent with the Muhammad costume was to make a comment about freedom of speech.

John   To point out that the culture this girl and so many other kids were supporting would not support their right to be at this party.

John Sr   The Muslim student group tried to shut down the party?

John   No – I mean the larger Muslim culture, which they weren't even talking about in their argument that certain speech should be banned from campus. It was like, if America says it, it's bad, end of discussion.

John Sr   So you were making an abstract point to your fellow students that if they defend Islam, they should know what kind of culture they're defending, in your understanding of it?

John   Nobody was defending Islam really – I mean, this is a really insular – it's college, it's, it was a Friday night, my friend and I were sitting around, Pastor Bob's book was out, this party was going on, there's been all this endless debate on campus about the cartoons . . . it just happened.

John Sr   I don't understand – now you're saying you didn't have any real intent in going to this party dressed as Muhammad?

John   No, just – I was frustrated, I was – this girl, she's like representative of – I'm surrounded by these privileged kids who attack everything American, who have nothing critical to say about any culture that they think we oppress. I'm sick of it, I'm sick of, I mean I'm critical of America too, but I'm sick of this decadent, these people who say America is bad but feel no responsibility to make it better, they just go off on it and get wasted and throw naked parties. It's not real, I feel like, it's like I'm surrounded all day by all these opinions just floating in the air that have no connection to the truth. I hate it, I'm fucking *sick* of it . . .

Pause.

John Sr   I hope the lines of communication are open between us.

John   They are.

John Sr   I know we haven't had much time together in the last year and a half –

John   You've been running for President.

Pause.

John Sr   I remember from our sessions with Dr Green that as a boy you sometimes felt I wasn't there for you, even though you were always on my mind –

John   We don't have to go through all this, I worked out my abandonment issues –

John Sr   Well, I only bring it up because tonight – sitting with my father has been a reminder of the gulf that can exist between a father and a son. Even when they appear to be close.

John   I don't feel a gulf.

Pause.

John Sr   I hope – if you did – you could tell me.

John   I could.

John Sr   I don't ever want anything to happen like what happened when you were sixteen. I couldn't bear to lose you. I love you.

Pause.

John   Thank you. I love you, too.

John Sr   Sitting with my dad, I was remembering our fishing trips – those trips we took, yours and mine . . . do you remember those?

John   Of course.

Pause.

John Sr   One thought I had about our relationship recently – I might be off-track with this, but humor me – I realized the other day that there was something I hadn't spoken to you about which I felt was regrettable.

Pause.

As you know, I support civil unions and antidiscrimination legislation – but my position, the position I took, on gay marriage – as I'm sure you know, I didn't support it in the campaign and what I said was, I personally didn't believe in it. In retrospect, I think I should have explained to you that the real reason I didn't support it is that I didn't think the country was there on this yet – in fact, we did extensive polling that was pretty conclusive about that. Someday the country will be ready – I'm certain it'll be in your lifetime – but first we need to take a compromise step to civil unions, which I plan to fight to achieve –

John   Okay – you said you don't have a lot of time, can we get to the pictures?

John Sr   Well – I don't have a lot of time, but this is important.

John   Just tell me what you want me to do.

John Sr   Why are you being snippy? I just want to make sure you understand – my position on gay marriage doesn't have to do with any homophobia on my part, or my playing to any homophobia that may be out there –

John   That might be easier to believe if you hadn't done that event with Pastor Bob.

Pause.

John Sr   Now why would that be?

John   He's the most influential evangelical in the country, and he makes it very clear that being gay is a sin and that gay people are going to hell.

You legitimized this man by appearing with him –

John Sr   Wait a second – he's been on every talk show, every magazine cover, he was already legitimate well before I –

John   You sent a signal that you're fine with his bigotry, that it's okay with you –

John Sr   That's not true – I didn't change a single position of mine in support of gay rights, or abortion rights, or anything at all, when I met with him. The signal I did send had to do with common ground – his church, as I'm sure you know, has done extraordinary work in Africa, with Aids –

John   As an excuse for evangelizing, for converting starving Africans to Christianity. He's trying to buy off governments in Africa so he can merge church and state –

John Sr   I don't know anything about that. His church is doing work on poverty, the environment –

John   Yeah, did you ever stop to think why? In interviews he talks about how the evangelical movement has been at the forefront of every American progressive battle – abolition, suffrage, civil rights – as if those are anything like the kinds of

movements he wants to be aligned with today. He wants to
legitimize his church and gain political capital so he can begin
to erode the separation of church and state –

John Sr   I think you're overstating it a bit, being a bit
dramatic, but trust me – there is no chance of that happening
under my watch. And I didn't meet with him because I agreed
with his positions on social issues, I met with him because he
is on the moderate end of the evangelical movement –

John   You met with him to *win votes* –

John   No – this is important – I met with him because I think
that whatever we can do to bring evangelicals a little closer to
the center is a good thing –

John   He's not going to move closer to the center, he's a
literalist, what's right is right and he knows it because God
told him. If anyone's going to get moved anywhere, it's going
to be you.

John Sr   You have my word that I'm not going anywhere.

John   You already did! You conveyed that what this man
stands for and preaches is okay – that people like me, like your
son, deserve to burn in hell.

John Sr   I've never heard Pastor Bob say anything remotely –

John   When the camera's rolling, he says it with a smile, in
code – he speaks in generalities about the authority of the
Bible. But in other places he says it directly, and he means it.
You have to have known this, I'm sure your campaign briefed
you –

John Sr   Let me tell you this: this election would have been
over for me a long time ago if I had not shown my willingness
to work with and be comfortable around all kinds of people.

John   Even people who condemn your son to hell.

John Sr   That's right. To be frank.

We're getting reports of riots in Pakistan. I'm sure you know
how sensitive things are –

John   What time is it in Pakistan?

John Sr   What time is it? I believe it's late morning or early afternoon.

John   That's a little fast, the pictures have only been online a couple hours –

John Sr   Are you saying you don't believe me?

Now, how do we respond? I want you to know, I'm very sensitive to your autonomy and your privacy, the things you and Dr Green determined were important for you in relation to my political life –

John   Not just 'important'.

John Sr   What?

John   I flipped my car over, I wanted to *die* –

John Sr   I'm saying that – look, don't bring that up like that –

John   You're talking about my autonomy like it's something we can negotiate in terms of how it impacts you. It's not just 'important', it's my life! I've worked so hard to become myself –

John Sr   I know that! I know what you went through! I went through it with you! Look, a lot of folks in the campaign wanted to do something unilaterally – and I said no – no decision involving my son happens without his consent. So if you don't want to do anything, that's fine with me . . . Can I just – is it impeding your autonomy to make a proposal? Which you are free to reject?

Pause.

I want to impress upon you the seriousness of this. Not in terms of my administration – there's always a political angle, I know you know that, I'm not talking about that, by tomorrow there'll be some other thing to supplant this. But in terms of the international situation – I've spent a lot of time studying this part of the world –

John   I have, too.

John Sr   I'm sure. I'm sure. Now maybe you've come to different conclusions than I have, but what I've determined, given what I know about Islamic culture – which isn't monolithic – you know what I – I don't have to go through all that. The bottom line is, to me, the most effective thing to do would be for you to put out, in your own words, a very brief statement of sincere regret and apology. And I think that'll be the end of it, and you can go back to school tomorrow and live your life. No big network interviews or photo ops with Muslims – a statement and that's that.

Pause.

John   My concern is, once I put out a statement I'll become a public person, and I'll never have privacy again.

John Sr   Actually, I think it's the reverse – if you don't put out a statement, the press won't leave you alone till you do. When it was just the pictures it might have blown over – but not with that video.

Pause.

I wrote something. Of course this would be in your own words –

John *reads.*

John   I don't feel this way.

John Sr   You can put it in your own –

John   I don't feel this way at all.

Pause.

John Sr   One of the challenges of this campaign was to build a foreign policy that would be strong as well as conciliatory. To show the Islamic world that we would defend our vital interests, but that there would also be a new era of respect. I know from our discussions that this is important to you as well. Now, if America appears to be disrespectful of a foundational aspect of Islamic society – I think that sends a poisonous message. And I don't see how we begin the work of finding common ground.

John   But I don't think we should give up our values to find common ground. Then it's not common ground, it's their ground, and we're just standing on it.

John Sr   What values am I asking you to give up?

John   If I take back what I did, I've given up my freedom of expression!

John Sr   No, you've just shown a little tact – don't use ideology to negate reality.

John   How is what I'm saying ideological?

John Sr   It's ideological in that you're making it about freedom of expression –

John   I'm not 'making' it –

John Sr   – when the reality is, this is about facts on the ground, and the facts on the ground are, if you don't demonstrate contrition, innocent lives may be lost!

Pause.

John   Innocent lives may be lost?

John Sr   As I'm sure you're aware.

John   If you want to talk about innocent lives being lost, then why don't we talk about your support of Israel.

Pause.

John Sr   The last thing we're going to talk about right now is Israel.

John   Of course it is –

John Sr   If you can't see the contradiction between your arguing for these rights that are so important to you and your sneering disdain for the only country in the Middle East that would grant you those rights –

John   Unless I'm a Palestinian, then my human rights don't look quite so secure –

John Sr   Look, it comes down to this: if you don't apologize –

John   – then people will die. I reject that. That is specious.
My putting on a turban is not responsible for people being
killed a half a world away –

John Sr   See, that's the – there's something you're missing
here, and it's interesting to me, because you're such a smart
guy. Do you realize what it is?

Pause.

John   What?

John Sr   A few minutes ago you were talking about Pastor
Bob – you were criticizing me for doing an event with him.
You said I legitimized him, and that bothered you. That
bothered you because you felt that that was something that
would have an effect, am I right?

John   He's – explicitly homophobic, yeah. You validated –

John Sr   I could say that what you did was explicitly
Islamophobic. You're saying that my appearing with Pastor
Bob sends people the message that the Democrats think it's
okay to not respect gay people, which will lead to *their* deciding
it's okay to not respect gay people. Now if you argue that, then
you have to also argue that your dressing up as Muhammad
sends people a very clear message that it's okay for them to not
respect Muslims as well.

Can you see that? I'm sure you can, it's very basic.

John   . . . The difference is, you're a nationally known
politician, I'm not.

John Sr   Wait a second – has it really not occurred to you at
any point tonight that you are the son of the President-elect
of the United States of America?

Pause.

Now I think you finally –

John   I'm not in a position to pass legislation affecting
millions of –

John Sr   Do you really not see? If you're Muslim and you feel beat up by the rhetoric that's been coming out of this country, and you see this video where the son of the next President is mocking your prophet in a homosexual fashion – Excuse me.

He reads a text.

John   When you needed to be conservative to get elected to Congress, you were conservative. When you needed to become more liberal to be viable nationally, you became more liberal. Whatever you've needed to be to win you've become, to the extent that no one actually knows who you really are or what you actually believe –

John Sr   You're changing the subject –

John   I'm trying to explain to you how we're different, because I don't think you understand a person who feels it's important to have convictions no matter what the circumstances are –

John Sr   We can argue about compromise versus convictions later, I'll be happy to debate you on that, but I think what's more pressing is that we've discovered here a contradiction you're not able to answer to –

John   I believe in my right to express myself –

John Sr   Regardless of the consequences – when it's you. With others, the consequences suddenly start to matter –

John   I'm not giving an apology.

Pause.

John Sr   I would think someone as intelligent as you would want to have a more sophisticated argument than what basically amounts to a temper tantrum.

John   I think freedom of expression is more than a temper tantrum.

John Sr   All right, what is this really about? Let's have this out –

John   It's about what I believe –

John Sr   No – you go to a party and act this way? On the eve of my *triumph* –

John   Right, it's all about you! What else would I expect from a narcissist who gives his son his own fucking name?

John Sr   What?

Naming you was an act of *love* – how *dare* you denigrate your name –

John Sr *attacks* **John.**

Jessica   John! –

John Sr   There are things in this world that are bigger than you –

Jessica   Stop!

Pause. Father and son look at one another. **John Sr** *goes.*

John's *phone rings.* **Jessica** *goes.*

John *takes his phone and goes into the bathroom.* **Matt** *opens the closet door. He goes to the TV.* **Marc** *enters.*

Marc   A long time since we won one of these.

A lot of people right now – just like us. Standing in front of their TVs. Makes you feel a part of something, right?

This is the country, whatever you can say about it, it's the one people want to come to, people want to be like, people look to . . .

Pause.

Matt   Not everyone . . .

Marc   No, not everyone, obviously. But all around the world right now, people are watching because, say what you will, America is this hope, this beacon. And now it's our turn to make her better. Not just for us, but for everybody, for the world. Even for the people who hate us.

What other country on earth can say that?

Pause. **John** *comes out of the bathroom.*

Marc   Hey, buddy. We're about to go out with this statement, I just wanted to run it past you.

Jessica *enters.*

Jessica   We're not going to put it out. I just talked to John.

We're going to sleep on it.

Marc   How many decisions are happening here –

John   It's fine. Put it out.

Dad said there were riots in Pakistan. I don't want anyone to get hurt.

Pause.

Marc   You want to look it over?

John   No.

Marc *goes.*

John   You called Dr Green?

Jessica   I thought you might want to speak to him.

Pause. **Jessica** *goes.*

John   That was weird, hearing his voice. All these years . . .

Matt   What did he say?

John   He said he understood what I was feeling, how it fits into my history . . . but I need to remember that other people have histories too . . . that they feel just as strongly about . . . and was there a way I could take everybody's histories into account . . .

He sits. Pause.

When the phone rang I was so sure it was Robbie –

He cries. Pause.

I'm starving. You want anything?

He goes to hotel phone.

Hi, I'd like to order room service. One filet, medium rare and – (*looks at* **Matt**) your most expensive vegetarian dish. And a couple beers, whatever you want to send up.

Don't charge it to the room, I'll pay cash.

Matt   It's so hard to think about this stuff. It's so huge . . .

Pause.

John   Did you hear that?

Matt   What?

John   They said he's expected any minute.

I don't think I can watch.

Matt   You don't have to.

Pause.

John   You can watch if you want.

He picks up his book. **Matt** *sits at his laptop.*

John   Did he come out?

Matt (*looks to TV*)   Not yet.

Pause.

Do you want me to tell you when he comes out?

John   It's okay, I'm just gonna read.

Pause.

Is that it?

Matt   He just came out.

John *puts down the book. Pause. He goes to the TV.*

John   There he is.

My whole life I've been picturing this moment . . .

Pause.

Matt   Are you okay?

John   I don't know what I am.

I guess I'm . . .

Proud.

Matt *and* **John** *look at one another.* **John** *looks away.*

Matt *turns to the TV.*

John *goes to the window, looks out.*

He opens the window. Sounds of thousands cheering.

Hold.

Methuen Drama Student Editions

Jean Anouilh *Antigone* • John Arden *Serjeant Musgrave's Dance*
Alan Ayckbourn *Confusions* • Aphra Behn *The Rover*
Edward Bond *Lear* • Bertolt Brecht *The Caucasian Chalk Circle*
Life of Galileo • *Mother Courage and her Children*
The Resistible Rise of Arturo Ui • *The Threepenny Opera*
Anton Chekhov *The Cherry Orchard* • *The Seagull* • *Three Sisters*
Uncle Vanya • Caryl Churchill *Serious Money* • *Top Girls*
Shelagh Delaney *A Taste of Honey* • Euripides *Elektra* • *Medea*
Dario Fo *Accidental Death of an Anarchist* • Michael Frayn *Copenhagen*
John Galsworthy *Strife* • Nikolai Gogol *The Government Inspector*
Robert Holman *Across Oka* • Henrik Ibsen *A Doll's House* • *Ghosts*
Hedda Gabler • Charlotte Keatley *My Mother Said I Never Should*
Bernard Kops *Dreams of Anne Frank* • Federico García Lorca
Blood Wedding • *Doña Rosita the Spinster* (bilingual edition) •*The House
of Bernarda Alba* • (bilingual edition) • *Yerma* (bilingual edition) • David
Mamet *Glengarry Glen Ross* • *Oleanna* • Patrick Marber *Closer* • John
Marston *The Malcontent* • Joe Orton *Loot* • Luigi Pirandello *Six
Characters in Search of an Author* • Mark Ravenhill *Shopping and
F***ing* • Willy Russell *Blood Brothers* • *Educating Rita* • Sophocles
Antigone • *Oedipus the King* • Wole Soyinka *Death and the King's
Horseman* • August Strindberg *Miss Julie* • J. M. Synge *The Playboy
of the Western World* • Theatre Workshop *Oh What a Lovely War*
Timberlake Wertenbaker *Our Country's Good* • Arnold Wesker *The
Merchant* • Oscar Wilde *The Importance of Being Earnest* • Tennessee
Williams *A Streetcar Named Desire* • *The Glass Menagerie*

Methuen Drama Modern Plays

include work by

Edward Albee
Jean Anouilh
John Arden
Margaretta D'Arcy
Peter Barnes
Sebastian Barry
Brendan Behan
Dermot Bolger
Edward Bond
Bertolt Brecht
Howard Brenton
Anthony Burgess
Simon Burke
Jim Cartwright
Caryl Churchill
Noël Coward
Lucinda Coxon
Sarah Daniels
Nick Darke
Nick Dear
Shelagh Delaney
David Edgar
David Eldridge
Dario Fo
Michael Frayn
John Godber
Paul Godfrey
David Greig
John Guare
Peter Handke
David Harrower
Jonathan Harvey
Iain Heggie
Declan Hughes
Terry Johnson
Sarah Kane
Charlotte Keatley
Barrie Keeffe
Howard Korder

Robert Lepage
Doug Lucie
Martin McDonagh
John McGrath
Terrence McNally
David Mamet
Patrick Marber
Arthur Miller
Mtwa, Ngema & Simon
Tom Murphy
Phyllis Nagy
Peter Nichols
Sean O'Brien
Joseph O'Connor
Joe Orton
Louise Page
Joe Penhall
Luigi Pirandello
Stephen Poliakoff
Franca Rame
Mark Ravenhill
Philip Ridley
Reginald Rose
Willy Russell
Jean-Paul Sartre
Sam Shepard
Wole Soyinka
Simon Stephens
Shelagh Stephenson
Peter Straughan
C. P. Taylor
Theatre de Complicite
Theatre Workshop
Sue Townsend
Judy Upton
Timberlake Wertenbaker
Roy Williams
Snoo Wilson
Victoria Wood